A
Warrior's
Way

Follow us on all
social media
accounts for
daily motivation
and updates

Title: The Warrior Code
Author: Eric Douglas Fliger

ISBN: 978-0-578-28229-9

@awarriorway on IG and tik tok, A Warriors Way on Facebook. awarriorsway.org

The Warrior Code Outline:

1. Faith (What you believe in)
2. Morality and Ethics (right vs. wrong, what is right)
3. Understanding/Caring (Why you believe, personal reflection)
4. Hardships/ (How to handle pain and suffering in life)
5. Respect (You have to give to get it)
6. Miracle of Love – love creates miracles
7. Integrity (Defining your character and its role)
8. Empower, Inspire, Unite (3 laws of a Warriors' Way)

Introduction:

What is the Warrior Code? These are the codes to set ourselves up for a better philosophy in life. Becoming a warrior in modern times is often a struggle because so many things influence and effect our daily lives. We often lose sight of our common core and personal strengths to fit in with society. Well, fear no more. This will be the guide to a better strength of daily mindsets that each of us can apply at all times. Sometimes the truth will piss us off before it sets a free. The Warrior sees through the "foo-foo of life," and is determined to justify what's right. Are you ready to become a Warrior? Do you want to be a better person for yourself and everyone else around you? Have you decided that you are done struggling with the average conformity that tries to shake you with every vulnerable chance? Each and every code will build you a better foundation of applicable wisdom. The world needs the warrior in you. I'm telling you right now that the world NEEDS YOU! No More Excuses.

1. FAITH

Are you ready for the challenge of the first code? Be prepared because everything you have ever learned may be put on the spot like never before. What defines your faith? This question may seem so simple, but it really is not. Do you know what you believe in, or have you just applied past education as your reasoning? Have we always just done what we are told, or have we thought about why things should apply to us. It's easy to say I believe in this, I believe in God, or I believe in myself. The issue becomes that we paint a portrait dream of what we believe in, but never stopped to realize that we actually are the artist of it.

"Well, I thought God is the everlasting artist to all things?"

Yes. Yes, He is. God also provided the tools necessary for us to create our image within Him and His creation. He created the world and all things in it. He created us, so we can add our own personal stamp and footprint. Regardless of how many times we fail to design our own dream, the portrait He supplied will always remain a beautiful constant. Thus, if we fail it is only because we believe more in the terror of fear, than we do the big picture. Fear happens and we all go through it at some point. The big picture constantly remains beautiful, but the process isn't always going to be that way. The world today tells us if we are not keeping up with trends and all things pretty, than we're not valued the same. The grits of life are the very reason we become beautiful. (Grits – Experiences and struggles that shape us) Our faith should be tested by these grits day in and day out. If we wish and yearn for a new found strength, than all things must be tested in the form that God decides to provide to our individual needs. Never get discouraged by what you see in front of you. Too many people are scared and fearful that if they show their grits, that their pretty reputations will be vulnerable. Think about it, if our faith is strong enough we would not worry much about our reputation. Our reputations should not be valued higher than our integrity. When we do this our vision becomes altered and compromised by selfish and destructive ways. When we lose faith, we lose integrity. This does not mean we should not care about how we look, or how others view us. There is sentimental meaning to both perspectives. The common theme or saying "You should not care what others think of you," is complete and utter nonsense. Seriously since when, is not caring a stronger core value? Please tell me. I'll wait. Not caring is an insecurity, a cop out, an escape, and loophole out of taking care of what needs cared for. It takes one of strong faith to stand up and announce that caring is important. The ability to truly care, but not let situations effect emotional stability is what strength looks like. In modern lehman terms, "not giving a f*ck" should actually be recognized as stronger emotional intelligence to overcome and adapt the adversity circling within our energy, versus the surface level of not caring at all vibes which hurt us more down the road.

Solution to Faith?

Faith should be a feeling more than a label. As mentioned in the beginning, a lot of people define their faith because they're just use to the system. Unfortunately, many use their faith one day a week – in church. Church has become a label to mask someone's full identity in their faith. The solution to faith is found when we engrave it in our souls, rather than a conversation piece. You should be able to have it without needing to converse about it. The expression "pay more attention to the quiet ones is right for a reason." A strong person doesn't feel like they need to promote it for attention. Instead, using their faith to balance their situational atmospheres in life tends to offer a better outcome. Learn to channel your faith through every-day life. Balance it every time something new or old presents itself to you. This will bring Morals and ethics into the mindset as well, which will be covered in another code of its own. Our faith should be enveloped in the way we talk, act, think, and feel. Faith is a 24-7 package that understands we're not perfect. It's a great feeling knowing God always has faith in us, but do we use that energy and channel it into our own belief system to? It's the Feeder Faith system. God has faith in us, and that should remind us of the strength allowed in our own self-belief system. Grow our faith, and it will plant the right seeds for our successes. It's better to believe in God and find out He's not real, than to not believe in Him and find out He is real. The glass should always be half full. We want to be hydrated and replenished with positive faith. A lack of faithful hydration leads to a depleted correlation of real and the spiritual. Look, even if whatever your life led to believe God is not real per say, why not use the pillar of positivity that He provides. It's beyond helpful, for that I promise you. The true people of faith do not Bible bang in your face, so do not let extremists of any culture or belief ruin it for those who truly mean well to you.

2. Morality & Ethics:

We have all been challenged many times that demands a swift reaction making our time for decisions very limited. Society is structured in such ways, that our choices will result in some outcome effecting what's around us. What did we do? Let's think to ourselves right now about some of the decisions we made that actually had a choice to make. I'm not referring to the times that we were uneducated about the consequences. Those can be out of our control as we have yet to receive the experience teaching us our lesson. It's worse if we know what's right, but decide to do otherwise. What makes us act out? Why do we choose to do wrong? If the energy used is the same or more, why not choose to do what's right? I understand everything is not so black and white. That is why I believe the gray area is the basis of morality and ethics. That moment of "What should I do?" occurs. The general conceptions of what is right and wrong take place in most of our thought processes before we act. It may only be a split second, but for that split second we know what's right or at least could be the better option. We must learn to control the virtue of free will while knowing we always have a choice. I understand this is personal perspective, but I'll allude to what makes us act in wrongful or evil ways. Early conditions have a way of absorbing our energy from a young age that causes to think and act wrongly. Our living situations, associations, environments, and surrounding energies give us a secondary response mechanism. It makes us consider what those things will think of us post decision. Will it make them think less of us because it's a direct opposite for the conditioned calling? Will it make them think we are weak? Will it cause internal conflicts that we cannot risk? Fear is a powerful device. Fear is a primal force that negates our right of mind. This force will take the greatest of greats and bring them down the worst evil in the world. It will batter us in ways causing internal hysteria and broken perspectives that make us seem there is no way out. We let fear take the steering controls of our life and forget the direction we were meant to cruise in. It happens to everyone us, and will continue to hit us when we least expect it. The devil works in many universal and creative ways, and does not mind taking us down when we believe we're at our highest. However, why you should not fear drowning in this thought of life is because you are not alone. We all go through this in one way or another. I know you're probably ready to throw the misery loves company vibe at me, and yes as that may always hold true; unity simply reacts by the energy we put into it. The focus you have in life will likely gravitate towards similar focuses flowing in that channel of unity. In short, what you think and believe will manifest itself around you sooner than later. It's a very precise and key decision to what we put in our minds, because it will become a daily influence whether it's in or out of our control.

Solution to Morality and Ethics?

It really boils down to what you want to be associated with. You can listen to the overwhelming thousands of words in your head stretching you every which direction, or you can close your ears and hone into that echo from within trying to carve its way into your very existent being. This is arguably one of the hardest feats in life is to arrive at this awakening, and moment of true deliverance.

We give ourselves choices daily. If we're not checking them and trying to decipher our own code to reality, than what is our existence really being manifested by? Are we being dragged along, or are pulling our own goals? That echo is the key to thriving your morality and ethical self. The ability to know on a general idea the difference of right and wrong, and decide on the best thing is the only true way even if it means sacrifice. We have to do this and catch ourselves doing this in a habitual manner every single day. Consistency and perseverance will slowly increase daily growth towards this goal of infinite morality and ethical appreciation. Good vs. Evil and Right vs. Wrong is always one decision to and from the next to determining what becomes of us. It was never meant to be easy, but true fortitude creates authentic gratitude.

3. Understanding and Caring

_We can sum this topic up into Empathy. It's one of the biggest players in developing relationships and establishing a true ability to be caring and understanding. Without empathy, we are almost lost souls in a universe where energy is constantly trying to unite us in some way or another; such as faith, love, inner connectivity down to a cellular level. I believe a foundational step to intrinsic growth should be instilled during youth. Teaching our young how to be more open and adhering to those talking to us, more than simply always be the ones talking. Anyone can listen, but not everyone chooses to hear well. This is where we need to sever selfishness form servitude. Selfishness will teach us that everything we do is for and only for our best interest alone. Servitude will teach us that giving without return is the most gracious attribute a person can have. Charity and Tything are also gracious attributes of high importance. They are pure and untouchable. Often times, those who are self servant also believe they're caring because they're tending to themselves. That could be the crack to the code of narcissism, or simply is the exact definition of it in real time. Once they're enlightened to their own self-centeredness, they enact on it and become aroused by the idea that caring and tending to themselves should also be by those around them. The difference with an "empath" here is that their servitude isn't to cater and tend to themselves. It is to care for those who need it even if they are not aware like the true classic narcissists among us. That battle will always be forever colliding. Empathy vs. Narcissism. Can we ever be caring and understanding enough to break that some time down the line? Will it take artificial interference to subdue that internal conflict? Is there ever actually a winner? Will the empath win, or the narcissist? Can humanity finally come together to bond these into one personality type to get the best of both - the confidence and genuine integrity? We ask ourselves these questions, but are we doing the diligent work to carve the truth into our souls? Anyone can read information, but it's what we do and how we respond with it in a functional world. That alone can reveal to us all the difference between caring and saying we care. If you actually care, eventually some type of action will show how you feel inside. We can take as many personality tests as we'd like, but if we're not choosing to be more understanding; this information just becomes a poster on the wall that we simply walk by every day.

Solution to Caring and Understanding?

Well, in the great complexity that we've caused life to grow into with the catalystic and uncontrollable technology era; simplicity often appears as an unsung champion to chase. What matters to you and your life? Does it play a role in how you develop and adapt within the culture you're living in? We have to break down the anatomy of our own personality, goals, environments, and associations that we "habitualize" ourselves into. When we break these things down we get simple examples of them all and how they play a role in our daily choices and perspectives to how we act and react. Social media causes so much disruption in personal studies because we're often caught studying everyone else with every chance we get. If we're always doing that how can be maximally be caring and understanding to ourselves? Break it all down. I'm not saying remove everything that releases instant dopamine, but figure out how to cut it out and use a little at a time to funnel into your own personal discovery to become a more caring person. Caring for yourself as an empath trait is extremely different than its counterpart because its all to better whats around you for the gain of the environment. Always a great way to sustain this solution is to get around those who bring out the best positive traits you've broken down in your own studies. Assimilate a team worth growing with and around, and execute on it daily. You wont have to feel like you're forcing accountability with them because the natural energy they possess in presence will produce plenty of soul power achieve what is sought after.

4. Hardships

If you're like most people, there is an emotional laundry shoot of pain and memories that we try to toss down in hopes to remove them from our burdened reality. It does not necessarily make us weak to try to set aside our issues in hopes of clearing our conscience to allow our focus to remain on what is in front of us. It's a natural defense mechanism, and often times we do not even realize we were doing it. Part of life and learning how the growth curve works inherently comes from pain, hardships, adversity, and unexpected speed bumps before us. Without the experience from loss, it would be even harder to quantify the comprehension of what really matters in life, and what has meaning to us in the long term. When pain happens, trauma is induced into our brains and we seek any

creative coping mechanism possible to fight it-
even previous better memories. Often times
our natural reflex is to go back to what seemed
better before, even though that will most likely
insert a prelude to the same situations. During
this, it is also learning new thing that we never
knew about ourselves. "You don't know until
you try it" theory is very applicable even in a
event of misfortune. "When you get knocked
down, keep getting back up." All of these
cliche sayings are intrinsically vital to our
extrinsic truth. Nobody obviously ever wants
to deal with hardships, because please God
spare us our sanity and let us just live ever so
peacefully, right? In the lovely gray area of life
though, that is how God delivers
understanding. We are given the ability to
make choices with free will, and what we do
with that will determine whether or not there is
learning consequence or good karma (and /or
both). In the end, it's important to know that

everyone handles these things in life
differently. Some with similar baselines, but
there is psychological conditioning at play
that we have to personally address in order to
get to the root of the hardship and beginning
of the solutions necessary. We often notice
that it's easier to help other people in
situations at times than it is to check ourselves
not following the same advice we had given. It's
a shape of perspective thing. The ability to
see from the outside in is helpful because we
often get caught in our own trance of
perspective, and forget how big the world is.
This isn't to diss our own viewpoints in our own
hardships because they're as important as
any. However, accepting outside perspectives
in addition to our own will be much better in
terms of seeking routes to better results and
peace. Fear not heeding advice from
outsiders, sometimes is makes us realize why

we were stuck inside.

Solution to our hardships?

Nobody knows to the extent of what our
hardships were like, like we do ourselves;
followed by close family and friends, and
people gifted with empathy and the ability to
truly relate to people and see within their soul.
I know that sounds crazy, like how are some
people just naturally gifted in that category?
Well, same way people are naturally gifted
throwing a baseball or remembering the entire
studies and quantum theories about the
world. We often tend to seek refuge in comfort
which makes it that much harder to overcome
the worst trials and tribulations. Learning to
catch ourselves in that very moment of
awakening is ideal. Do we go back to what

we've already done or places that lead to that, or do we take this opportunity to use our current pain and embrace it with inspiration for tomorrow? Evaluate how the pain shapes you today. See what it can do as far as creating a perspective that benefits your vision in life to either help others and yourself. Often times, giving a hand to someone else even in the darkest times actually becomes the truth and light needed to overcome all adversity. It'll create connection that continues to lead you towards an internal salvation. Write down who, what, and all the why's of your pain. Begin to filter them out in what's provided mutually between each other. If it does not benefit and satiate your soul, it's probably best to move on and get rid of it. Do not fully burn bridges though because we all grow at different rates, and we will never know what someone can do for us and vice versa down the road. What do you want out of life?

What do you want out of your relationships? Have you healed yet, and are you working on it? Sometimes we never heal from past experiences and carry it into new ones and wonder why they don't work out. Seek Active Healing to move into a state of growth and overcoming adversities. Nobody can decide what is best for you all the time, despite heavy advice given. Absorb all the information about becoming better from others doing better, and let it be a guide to where you want to develop yourself. Your destiny resides in your ability to manifest the action and growth that our souls yearn for us.

5. Respect

This may be a pillar and the foundation rock of a kinetic wholesome life. In order to get respect, one must be giving it. I know you've heard it a million times, but there is so much truth to it. For an example, if we are simply expecting respect at all times based on our titles, finances, riches, wealth, etc it is not respect that we are being given. What is it then? Well, it's somewhat rather of a phantom disconnect. It's probably coming from a place of fear or envy. Respect pushes people who do it into other people with respect as well. Simply put, the lack of caring or understanding gratitude develops into disrespect. Conditioning may be a huge contributing factor on this. We can learn the utmost respect from those who continually give and seek gratitude unto others without the benefits or rewards returned. Do you want respect returned? We all do. Of course. It's one of the most pure forms of tenured love by life itself. I suggest giving it as often and genuinely as possible. You're not only setting yourself up for better relationships, but you're also inspiring others to do the same. Our circumstances, environments, and conditioning will all accumulate into perspectives of what our level of respect may look like at scale, because that's exactly how we were exposed to it. For example, someone may have been treated just poorly at home their whole lives to justify their own actions into adulthood. At least that is what they think to themselves because they do not know any better yet, and this often gets passed down to many generations. This all ties into a phantom disrespect towards ourselves that can branch into some pretty problematic situations of trauma in life. Some of these traumatic psychological wounds never heal and reflect unto others, which we can all agree triggers poor relationships- or simply just breaks them. I believe we are all guilty by association with this idea of traumatic psychology, because there are so many variables happening differently from household to household and cyber accounts to cyber accounts. Someone from a stable home and without worries of ever losing a pillow or plate at night may not understand respect the same someone who always has to scrape to get both would. They can say they understand and try to empathize, but it is only a piece of truly understanding. I believe this is all very key and nutrient dense to developing a peculiar comprehension of how respect can differ and plays a vital role in conditioning. There will always be major and lighter differences at play, and finding that middle ground of relatability can be very tough and crucial in order to truly understand others from different backgrounds. I would say there is more likeliness that more backgrounds are similar than not, until they are more broken down into diversities. When we we look at things as a whole we tend to mirror it the same at scale, but when we really dig into what individualizes us all it really begins to open the playing field of diversity; which is where we really see more light and beauty of life's specific natures. If you're constantly finding yourself rooted in a field of disrespect sometimes we have to look further back than just what is around us in the present time and setting. Why? Well, because that conditioning of a prior life is layered pretty thick and coated over many of times if it is never brought to our attention, resolved, or have been redeemed within ourselves by becoming to its own light.

Solution to Respect Deficiencies?

Again there will never be an exact solution for everyone identically. However, I do believe if we can shape some principles before pride or even passion, than we can set ourselves up for a greater result shaping respect around and in our lives. We must strive at all times be willing to deliver respect first. RESPECT MUST BE EARNED, is often a two way street depending on the way its digested. Yes, it should be earned but the missing idea there is that is has to be given by you to be earned for you. Never expect it to just randomly be delivered to your doorstep, bank account, job, pants pocket, neighbor, best friends, or even your husband and wives. Heck, even your parents as well. There must be a cultured yearning deep inside to want to provide respect to all of those mentioned above first. That is the true way for self redemption to feel the deliverance meant to manifest itself within us. I don't want to beg you, but if I had to beg you to try and manipulate some daily habits in hopes to secure better energy for you tomorrow, it's that I hope you try to give all respect that you can even if it hurts you for a prolonged period of time. It's better than hurting forever to never find out. Yes it may take more work, and yes it may require extreme focus, but the amount of energy output one way or the other will be the same - so why not use it all to positively run the score of our own life up. Respect the game, and not only will the game respect you; but it'll also bring you to better people, places, and things that will fill you with more respect along the way.

6. Miracle of Love

Speculation has it that miracles are not real. They are merely a figment of our overactive and imaginative over thinking processes. I guess this is one of those touchy topics where faith and science may differentiate. I see no reason why faith and science cannot work together and coexist to craft a stronger bond to truth and enlightenment. Why else have both available, and just neglect that human opportunity to be able to crack that code? We are so intelligent and emotionally understood as far as evolution goes in comparison to other species, and yet sometimes it's almost like we act like the most ungrateful species ever. Is there a lost miracle in that? Are we so deeply integrated and sunken into our own rationality and logistics that we cannot even see the outside of the box we're buried in? Possibly. Yet, every day we still see amazing transformations. Every day plants sprout new flowers. Every day the sun continues to warm our hearts. Every day the moon decides to control the tides so we don't have watch our beloved lands become ocean bottom and a new play pen for sea creatures. It's amazing to me how adaptive life forms can be, and still continue to be exuberant about growing again and again. This all may seem somewhat irrelevant to what miracles are, but I promise it has a primal role. It's a primitive role because there is energy around us, within us, and in all things that work acts of miracles every day before we have a chance to blink or think. Think about how functional the earth has to be before we can even exist and produce everything we have to offer. Is that not just wild and intense to think about?! It seriously blows my own mind thinking about how many things have to be just right and enforced with precision before we even wake with a yawn and fulfill it with a smooth cup of coffee. Tell me how that is not one form of a miracle? It seems quite astonishing to me. I do challenge your mind to go down the rabbit hole. Remove all egos, prejudices, mindsets, and previous preset points of views. Now walk outside and force yourself to see the beauty in the elements. If you don't see it maybe you're not looking hard enough, or not in the right frame of reference. Let it consume you. Be one with it. This may sound crazy, but talk to it as if it were another human. Constructive learning with the energy that infinitely surrounds us creates this precious gem of a spine chilling moment that allows gratitude to become overwhelming. That is a tell all time of our lives. Remember that moment. Cherish it. We may not be able to place the exact serenade of it that gave us our deliverance, but it will always be with us in all that we do. Now onto the juicy relationship human-to-human end of this. You want a miracle? To feel it so deep we can feel our toes tickle, and experience that overall shiver sensation. That my connected soul pals, is love. Love is the miracle you wish to find. It's really not that cliche. Everyone wants love and everyone some time will desire a miracle, so how is that not cliche you may ask. Imagine you're doing push-ups and you fail after only doing nine. Four weeks later you are able to do twenty! Four months later you can do thirty five push-ups, and a year later you are doing over fifty to sixty in one set. You never knew you could do all of those because all of that energy and work has never been compiled and snow balled yet. You only knew and thought about what you had so far. Slowly and surely adaptations allowed for progress to happen before your eyes. Now what if I told you that Love works the same way. A little love for four days. More love for four more weeks. Four months later your entire world seems to be filling with an abundance of love by taking positive actions every single day to enhance that. A year later comes around, and boom guess what? Everything happening now is a miracle compared to what never seemed possible on day one. Utter shock and awe takes over with every breath we take now, because we know every time we exhale someone else is inhaling the love we created. Therefore i lay testament to Love and only love being a finite source, the most abundantly dynamic, and quantifiable explanation behind how miracles are formed.

Solution to finding Love and its miracle

It is more simply said than it is done. First, we must place purpose, passion, and principles over pleasure, pessimism, and pain. The ability to consolidate them into separate groups will provide the catalyst to over coming the lack of love we feel void of. Write down somewhere right now before you go further. On one side write Purpose, Passion, and principles, and on the other write Pleasure, Pessimism, and pain. Under each category begin to write things related to each of them that are in your life- for each one also write their causes. With all of these things in front of you on paper it'll allow to see some focal points that need addressed, removed, and pushed harder on. In order to reach the next level in life in route to love we must play the hypothetical game of jenga and tetris with each piece being life, and how we choose to strategically place them. It clears space and opens doors for the Miracle to begin its inner workings to fulfill its existence in our lives. For example, if you fill a cup with water to the top and then try to add fruit to it it'll spill over. However, if you have clear space to place the fruit in first and then add in the water after it seems to work better doesn't it? This is often what we have to do with our lives first before the miracles tend to take place. God gave us the ability to do so, and with that we must strive towards giving Him and his elements of love a better place to reside in. It takes hard work no doubt. It takes admirable heart and will to overcome the sands of time weighing us down, but when we do. Oh, when we do. Life's purpose tends to become our prevailing gravity. If you want a miracle(s), you must be the love present at all times.

7. Integrity

When you look at someone in hindsight years down the road there is usually some type of taste left in our thoughts. How was the relationship formed and bonded with said person? Were we really connected as friends and closely knit, or was it simply just an association? Did they leave an impact on me, or did I leave one on them? Did they lead with their invigorated souls, or just go with the flow? These questions can be endless and abundant. I frame this part of the guide specifically so we can think about talking to the future version of ourselves, as well as the future versions of those around us. What would we say to each other forty years down the road? Was it a life of uncertainty, or full of integrity? It is meaningful and transpiring to really think about these things. Whether you're sitting in your cold and barren basement right now, or sleeping on a comforter made of gold and french silk. There's two forms of us left after we are gone. The legacy we leave to the world and how they remember us, and how our last thoughts of who we became shape our souls as they exit this physical world. Both should be important to our frame of purpose every single day. If we want integrity we have to strive to be passionate, charismatic, kind, grateful, and always forgiving -but never forgetting. Nobody is coming to save us the way we may have been conditioned to expect. It's a harsh reality, but it cognitively puts us in a complacent spiraling hole and void. Nobody can give us a life of integrity. We must take our diamond and begin to carve away the surfaces hiding our talents. We must work hard and give unto the world more than we want the world to give to us. Every positive action sets forth a pedestal for another one to begin. It's in these "wax on, wax off" moments that integrity is introduced and bonded. Every day we get to decide if our today will make our tomorrow more meaningful. Will our tomorrow make our next week empowering. Will our destiny be worth calling upon, or did we just sit there and collect information. In order to fulfill a legacy of integrity we must strive to provide kindness, gratitude, and our truth every single breathing moment we get. That isn't to say we have to be perfect, but in defining times there should be a switch that is flipped with wanting to do more; and to do it the most beneficial and right way possible. When you look into someones eyes are you looking for what they can give you, or are you focusing into their soul to see how you can help them give to the world? That has to remain an important focus, regardless how cruel the world and some people may seem. Remember, forgive but never forget. Another important thing I also believe in, is to never burn a bridge. You're giving them power because they just controlled your emotions. We also do not know what the future holds. Sometimes we can plant a seed now, and it not grow until down the road when we least expect it in another phase of life. These are all pieces that can build up to create a stronger character and integrity at heart.

Solution to Integrity?

I believe the magic in this one is to simply do more than watch. It's easy to sit on the sidelines and watch others live their lives, but at some point we have to get our ass up and put the game on our backs. Find great mentors who can be your Brett Favre to Aaron Rodgers. (it's a football reference where Aaron remained under legendary quarterback Brett until it was finally time to shine). Get up every day with purpose to make life better. Even if you do not know what you want to do or how you want to do it, it starts with getting up. Lift your mind, body, and soul towards somethings that lights a fire under your feet. You may even revert back to a past-time to hone in on what part of that made you happy, excited, or motivated. Once you do that you begin to really grasp the wisdom behind the passion once had, and can use it as a starting block. Get creative. Nobody is the same as far as what they can thrive at. You have something that will make your integrity stronger than you think. Own it. Be a better person than you forgot you were. One of the best lines i've ever heard was "Do not put off tomorrow what you can do today." That includes working on yourself internally where most people cannot, or will not see and help with. That's where optimal strength lies; within the shadows of unknown and the sacrifice it takes to work on ourselves while being there. Integrity is doing good work over time creating a habit that becomes an unstoppable monster. The good kind of monster obviously. We could get going down into complexities, but everyone's monster is very individualized, and that would require one on one manifestation and coaching.

8. Empower, Inspire, and Unite

This is the code. The three pillars of what we stand for. Becoming a warrior in life is more than advocating for good things, and laying claims to the belief in God. Anyone can go to church once a week, get a bible verse tattoo, put their favorite verse in the description of their social media profiles, but is that really what's happening behind the scenes? Often times we are present in an evolution of smoke and mirrors with the way we have adopted social media so quickly. Technology is moving so much faster than our brains can often handle and process at the same time. This tends to cause the desire to "fit in, go with the flow, and be absorbed by all things hyped and trendy." The issue with this is that it is absorbing the youth before they can even explore their own capabilities and talents. If you notice those who are content in their niche do not often need to try to fit in, unless their niche is surrounded by current trends and hype. In that case, they often have to lean on it to help build their niche or brand. Today, the internet doubles as a good and bad means of exposure. It can really expose the good things happening in the world, but it can also expose the bad at a level so quick it is often hard to decipher what even is good or bad. News flowing at you and whoever gets information to you the quickest believes that they are right, and when us people become a product and victim of that; it causes extreme hysteria and anxiety. When it forces us to think faster than we can our minds tend to default and just accept what hits us quickest; and therefore pay the consequences later. It's honestly a hard bitter pill to swallow just thinking about how we've become a literal consumable product. That is why we are here. We have to break this plane and transition of human evolution so technology and humanity don't ruin each other. Think about this? What do we do if we want inspiration? We run right to the internet and forego remembering what our actual talent and strengths are. After we've searched for a strong moment we get sucked into doing what everyone else is doing; and not that that does not hold value - it does, but we can't forget what our burning desires are at the same time. It's very complicating now. It is by no means an easy walk in the park today without getting absorbed into the meta reality. Now, again, do not get me wrong, there is a lot of really really great motivational and leadership influencers out there that are really shaping minds in a positively vulnerable way. Before all else though, what makes you you? That voice in your gut is not always just anxiety to make you feel helpless, it is to be your compass. It's an actual voice. You are not totally crazy (haha). It builds up when we do not act out what our soul is yearning for, and then it turns into a medical nightmare with doctors shoving pills and pills down our thoats until we are hypothetical zombies. Write these things down! All those voices. The warrior within you is waiting on action. It's all execution. It took me even way longer than it should to write this little self help guide due to self doubt and uncertainty of credibility. Everybody goes through this on their own timeline and experience, so you are not alone. I promise you, you are NOT alone! It's time for all of us Warriors to stand and rise for those who cannot themselves. You never know who is watching you. Your worst day could be viewed as a dream day for somebody else. Gratitude can carry our passions and empathy a long way. Are you grateful for your own life though? You should be, because every second you are breathing you are telling the world that you can bring value to it. Did you know that? The time is now! It may not be easy to thrive in your talents or grow your goals, and you may have the biggest setbacks ever. However, it is way better to always keep trying and pushing through the darkest times versus just letting the darkest times win so easily. Why waste the energy you are already using? I'm telling you that you can do this. Honestly, it can be quite the blessing because if you reading this have hit a true rock bottom it allows you to see the world on a much bigger spectrum. Why? Because you can see more from the bottom! I know, crazy! Empower yourself, Inspire that to the world. Unite with those who believe in you and your mission. Every failure is one step closer to a better one. Fail -fail - fail - succeed - fail ten more times - succeed two more- fail fifty more times- succeed forever more. There is no perfect circle and equation, but the one synonymous factor and variable is you never giving up!

Solution to Empower, Inspire, Unite

What do you want from life? I know one of my biggest desires and motivations is wanting to help inspire and empower others who have been to the lows of life. What is yours? Can you think of times after you did something and it made you feel really good or excited? Something positive that motivated you to want to do more good even though you may not have via not knowing what to do next. We've all been there, but we have to decide right now to be serious about our convictions and choices. You may not know if it is the right decision right away, but making one is one step closer to the right one. Nobody ever really tells us this. Making a decision to start a business or a job may turn into one hundred decisions that ultimately lead you to a whole other business or job that is way more successful! You have to make that decision to give it full go though. Without that execution and internal belief before you see the results, it will never get anywhere. Get around other people who make decisions all the time because you will learn to be vulnerable and deal with consequences of vulnerability and humility. Both very key ingredients to becoming a much better reinvention of ourselves. It is never too late to create the new you. Never. Its not pretending that the old you never existed or is not still there, but it's executing on a version that you know will get you to a better place and eating at a table with those that will help you thrive versus those who just tolerate acceptance. Do that! You are the solution, so let this be your extra little push and boost! I'm trying to keep this all very simple and straight to the point as there is no magic bullet to success if you are anything like me. A broken home bandit learning as I go. There is much beauty to be captured in that essence though, so embrace it! Turn it into something magical and profound so that the world can see you empowered, inspired, and united it! Do you think a flower knows what it's going to look like as a seed? Probably not, but even if it did look at what it turned into. You are the flower. Now imagine hundreds of flowers together because you inspired it. Life is literally like fireworks. People will stare at you whether you stay in a box on the shelves doing nothing, or they will be amazed at you when you shoot off into the night sky claiming your destiny and dreams in the clouds. What do they remember most? The crazy colors of personality and success flying all over the place. That is you! Do not be the person chilling on a shelf, be the person designing their life so that moment of glory can be captured everywhere, but most importantly felt by you! Quench your soul my friend. Honor your word. Create your Kingdom of life, and let God help instill every ounce of will needed to bind you to growth and empowerment. Rise Warrior, Rise!!!!

Time to Warrior Up!

This will be an exercise section for every part of the warrior code written in this guide. I want you to sum up in one paragraph of each section as if you were to write it to someone you would want to inspire. That could be a friend, family member, associate, or even yourself ten years down the road.

You are putting yourself in my shoes now becoming the adventurous writer! Half the battle is executing remember? Anyone can just read and intake information, but the real magic happens when we put it real use and work.

1. Faith (What you believe in)

2. Morality and Ethics (right vs. wrong, what is right)

3. Understanding/Caring (Why you believe, personal reflection)

4. Hardships/ (How to handle pain and suffering in life)

5. Respect (You have to give to get it)

6. Miracle of Love – love creates miracles

7. Integrity (Defining your character and its role)

8 . Empower, Inspire, Unite (3 laws of a Warriors' Way)

I will also leave pages for additional notes, self reflections, and journaling opportunities as well. Write down anything you're thinking in this very moment, or any time you get a relatable creative vibe, grab this guide, and write down things you know will help you. I would also like for you to send these in to me at: info@awarriorsway.org

Leadership and personal coaching is available as well.

If you are ready to take the next step from this guide and need more please inquire at

Awarriorsway.org
Info@Awarriorsway.org

Empower
Inspire
Unite
The Warrior Code

My warrior journey

Use this section to write
down all of your thoughts,
feelings, focuses, steps,
and constructive growth
towards a better and
stronger you

_____

Your ◆ name

_____

Date

Made in USA - Crawfordsville, IN
78366_9780578282299
05.06.2022 1737